by Douglas Steensland
in collaboration with
James Ployhar

To the Student

Level III of the Belwin "Student Instrumental Course" is a continuation of Levels I and II of this series or may be used to follow any other good intermediate instruction book. It is designed to help you become an excellent player on your instrument in a most enjoyable manner. It will take a reasonable amount of work and CAREFUL practice on your part. If you do this, learning to play should be a valuable and pleasant experience.

Please see the top of Page 4 for practice suggestions and other comments that should be very helpful.

To the Teacher

Level III of this series is a continuation of the Belwin "Student Instrumental Course", which is the first and only complete course for individual instruction of all band instruments. Like instruments may be taught in classes. Cornets, Trombones, Baritones and Basses may be taught together. The course is designed to give the student a sound musical background and, at the same time, provide for the highest degree of interest and motivation. The entire course is correlated to the band oriented sequence.

Each page of this book is planned as a complete lesson, however, because some students advance more rapidly than others, and because other lesson situations may vary, lesson assignments are left to the discretion of the teacher.

To make the course both authoritative and practical, the books in Level III are co-authored by a national authority on each instrument in collaboration with James Ployhar.

The Belwin "Student Instrumental Course" has three levels: elementary, intermediate and advanced intermediate. Each level consists of a method and two or three supplementary books. Levels II and III each have four separate correlated solos with piano accompaniment. The chart below shows the correlating books available with each part.

The Belwin "STUDENT INSTRUMENTAL COURSE" - A course for individual and class instruction of LIKE instruments, at three levels, for all band instruments.

EACH BOOK IS COMPLETE IN ITSELF BUT ALL BOOKS ARE CORRELATED WITH EACH OTHER

METHOD
"The Flute Student"
For Individual or Class Instruction.

ALTHOUGH EACH BOOK CAN BE USED SEPARATELY, IDEALLY, ALL SUPPLEMENTARY BOOKS SHOULD BE USED AS COMPANION BOOKS WITH THE METHOD

STUDIES AND MELODIOUS ETUDES

Supplementary scales, warm-up and technical drills, musicianship studies and melody-like etudes, all carefully correlated with the method.

TUNES FOR TECHNIC

Technical type melodies, variations, and "famous passages" from musical literature for the development of technical dexterity.

FLUTE SOLOS

Four separate correlated solos, with piano accompaniment, selected and arranged by Douglas Steensland:

The Magic Flute   *Mozart*
Hungarian Dance No. 6...*Brahms*
Offenbach Ballet   *Offenbach*
Themes from La Traviata...*Verdi*

CORRELATED FLUTE SOLOS

THE MAGIC FLUTE
W. A. Mozart — Arr. by Douglas Steensland

HUNGARIAN DANCE NO. 6
J. Brahms — Arr. by Douglas Steensland

OFFENBACH BALLET
J. Offenbach — Arr. by Douglas Steensland

THEMES FROM LA TRAVIATA
G. Verdi — Arr. by Douglas Steensland

FLUTE FINGERING CHART

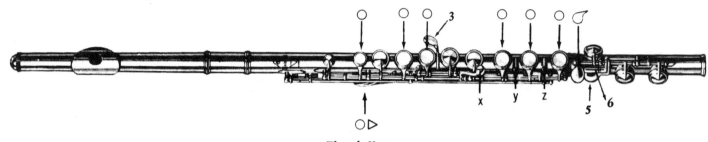

Thumb Keys

When a number is given, refer to picture of the instrument for additional key to be pressed.

When two ways to finger a note are given, the first way is the one most often used. The second fingering is for use in special situations.

When two notes are given together (F♯ and G♭), they are the same tone and, of course, played the same way.

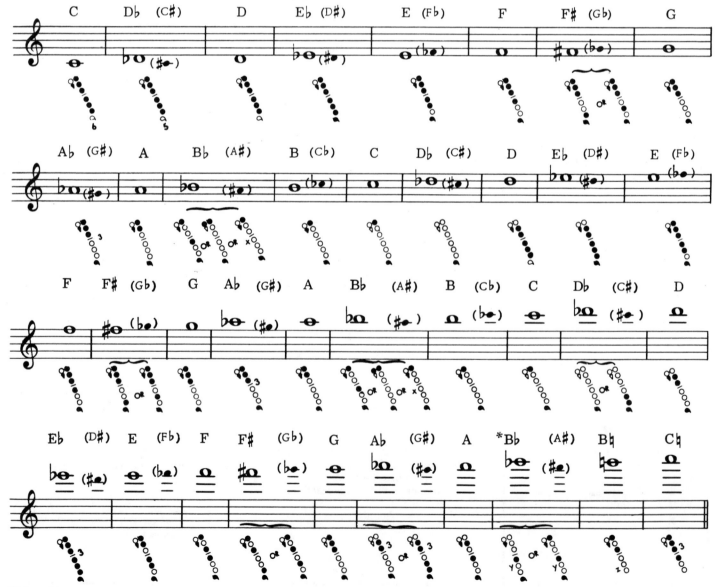

High B♭ may respond better with right little finger up.

TRILL CHART

See explanation of trills on page 42. For trills not shown on this page use the regular fingerings.

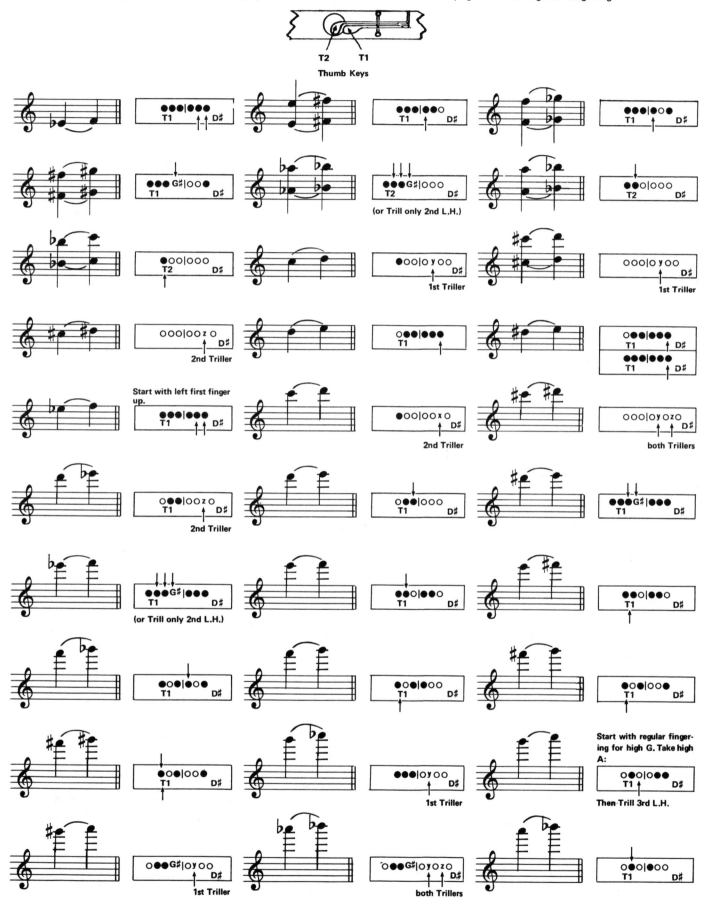

Note: When playing the right hand triller keys (y and z) use the third (middle) finger on key y and the fourth finger on key z.

4

A Few Important Practice Suggestions

1. Set a regular practice time and make every effort to practice at this time.

2. ALWAYS practice carefully. Careless practice is a waste of time. Learn to play each line exactly as written. COUNT AT ALL TIMES.

3. The development of careful and accurate playing habits is essential if you are to become a good player. Proper hand, finger, mouth or embouchure and body positions are absolutely necessary for best results.

4. Devote part of each practice session to playing by ear: scales, intervals (thirds, sixths, and octaves), arpeggios, and melodies. Play simple melodies and then transpose them into other keys.

5. Do at least half of your daily practice in a standing position.

Daily Warm-Up Studies

The lines below are for use as daily warm-up drills and should be used in addition to the regular lesson assignment. Also use the basic technic patterns on page **44**.

1. Hold each note as long as possible, maintaining best quality. Do this at various dynamic levels.

2. Play each tone using various shadings as indicated in (A), (B), and (C)

Also use low Eb, E♮ or F as the basic note and continue chromatically as shown. Work for a perfect legato and listen carefully to intonation.

Articulation

Play the above warm-up in all the keys you know.

If you have not already done so, please see the book "STUDIES AND MELODIOUS ETUDES FOR FLUTE", Level III, for more scale and technical studies that correlate with Method Book III.

Octave Slurs

Practice very slowly, then gradually increase tempo.

ARTICULATION REVIEW

Etude In G Minor

Etude In G Major

Air From "Water Music"

HANDEL

6

Please see the book "TUNES FOR FLUTE TECHNIC", Level III, for more melodies that provide for further technical development.

Study In Dynamics

1st time **pp** - **p** - **mp** - **mf** - **f** - **ff**
2nd time **ff** - **f** - **mf** - **mp** - **p** - **pp**   *simile*

Use various articulations.

First, play with two flats in key signature - then one sharp (g minor and G Major).

Practice each pattern with various articulations.

Articulation Etude

Sonata Theme

MOZART

B.I.C.301

Review the list of correlated solos listed at the top of Page 2.   These interesting solos were written specifically for this course and will enhance the study of your instrument. We suggest that you supplement your lesson assignments with one of these solos at all times.

TONE STUDY

Slowly

Start with your finest quality - then try to match this with each successive note.

CHROMATIC SCALE

*Be sure left first finger is up!

Legato - Staccato Etude

Moderato (in 2)

Arkansas Traveler

Allegretto

8

FINGERING TIP:
Keep fingers slightly curved at all times, in a natural, relaxed position, with pads of fingers over center of keys.

Scale Study In D Major

Waltz Etude

Berceuse From "Jocelyn"

GODARD

*See explanation on page 25.

Staccato Study

Etude In D Major

FINGERING TIP:
Keep right thumb under F key or slightly toward E key.

Low Register Etude

Romany Life

V. HERBERT

f minor *(Harmonic Form)*

f minor *(Melodic Form)*

Arpeggios

Use various articulations.

Maintain evenly divided eighth notes and triplets.

ABBREVIATIONS

Londonderry Air

TRADITIONAL

Andante espressivo

Count: &   4   &

slower

12

FINGERING TIP:
Always use the correct fingering for notes in the high register.   Any other fingering will affect the tone quality.

Scale Study In A♭ Major

Triplet Etude In G Minor

High Register Etude

Key Of A Major

OCTAVE SLURS
Slowly

1

2

A MAJOR SCALE

ARPEGGIO

3

Use various articulations.

CHROMATIC SCALE

4

Also slur.

Chord Study

In two

5

Also play with other articulations.

Triplet Etude

Moderato

6

Intermezzo From "Carmen"

BIZET

Andantino quasi allegretto

7

espressivo

See page 43.

Tone Study In Sixths

Also practice in 𝄵 and ¢ without holds.

Also slur.

Chromatic Triplets

Staccato Study

Moderato

Compare measures 1 and 3.   Play all rhythms accurately.

Rhythm Etude

FINGERING TIP:
Have left wrist bent enough to keep fingers over the G and G♯ keys.

OCTAVES

Scale Study In G Major

Syncopation Study

Viennese Melody

Tone Study

Slowly

①

② **4 or ¢** (a) (b) (c)

Play each of the above several times, with various articulations.

Legato Study

Andante (in 3)

③

espressivo

Compare these two lines:

④ **This rhythm is frequently played as indicated below.**

Play the sixteenth notes very lightly.

Humoresque

TSCHAIKOWSKY

Allegretto

⑤ *mf* *p*

f

f p *f* *p*

f *f*

Key Of D♭ Major

Practice ①, ② and ③ with various articulations.

Etude In C Minor

Allegretto

The Trout

SCHUBERT

Allegretto

B.I.C.301

FINGERING TIP:

Always keep right little finger on D♯ key except for these notes:

*optional

Practice with various articulations.

Count: 1 2 3 1 2 3 1 2 3

Scale Study In B♭ Major

Pastorale

SCHANTL

Andante (in 3)

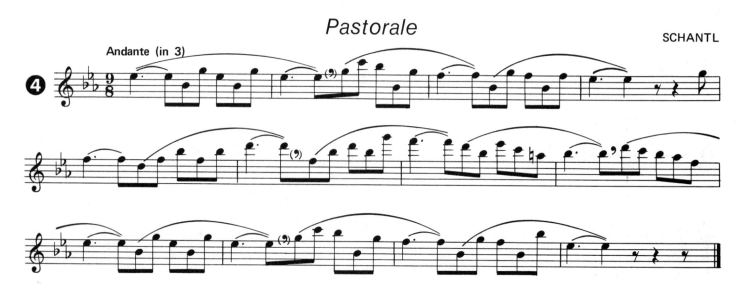

B.I.C.301

b minor *(Harmonic Form)*

b minor *(Melodic Form)*

Etude In B Minor

Allegretto

Chromatics

Also tongue

Also tongue

Serenade

SCHUBERT

Slowly

*Tongue in a soft, legato style.

TONE STUDY

Slowly

Scale Study

First play with five flats - then with two sharps (D♭ Major and D Major)

ABBREVIATIONS

Rhythm Etude

Practice in both 6 beats and 2 beats per measure.

Theme From "Fifth Symphony"

Andante con moto

BEETHOVEN

f# minor *(Harmonic Form)*

f# minor *(Melodic Form)*

Arpeggio

Use various articulations.

Work up to fast tempo.

Comparing 6/8 And 12/8

Theme From "Fifth Symphony"

TSCHAIKOWSKY

Andante cantabile (♩.= 54)

KEY OF E MAJOR

Scale Study In E Major

Theme From "Poet And Peasant Overture"

SUPPÉ

SYNCOPATION IN ¢

Theme From "Prometheus Overture"

(Duet)

BEETHOVEN

TONE STUDY

Rhythm Study In E Major

Scale Etude

Practice first in 3 beats per measure.

The above etude may also be played in D Major.

Solveig's Song

EDVARD GRIEG

Slowly

1 Tongue all notes the first time. On the repeat slur as indicated.
Be sure all D flats are in tune. Avoid the natural tendency to go sharp on this note.

simile

2 (a) (b) (c)

Practice each pattern with various articulations.

Legato Etude

Moderato

3 Practice both ways. *sim.*

Fine

rit. - - - - - - - - - - - - - - - -

D. C. al Fine

La Raspa

MEXICAN DANCE

Moderato

4 *mf*

f *p*

Fine *f* *mf*

f *mf*

3 *3*

* 8va

3 *3* *f* *3* *3*

D. C. al Fine

*Practice this section in both octaves.

Play both ways in the two keys indicated.

Octave Etude

Moderato

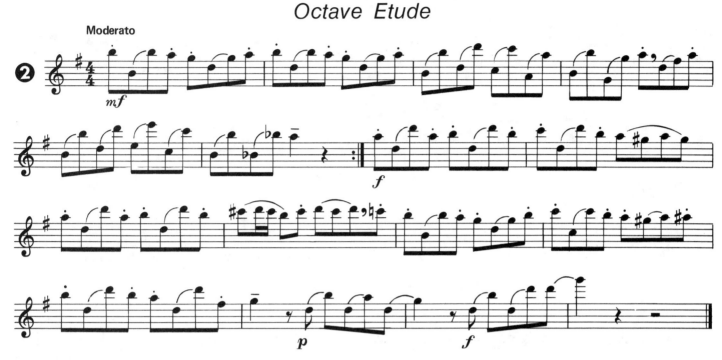

Since a dot placed after a note adds one-half of its value, two dots placed after a note will add one-half plus one-quarter of its value.

As written:

As played:

March Pontificale

GOUNOD

Maestoso

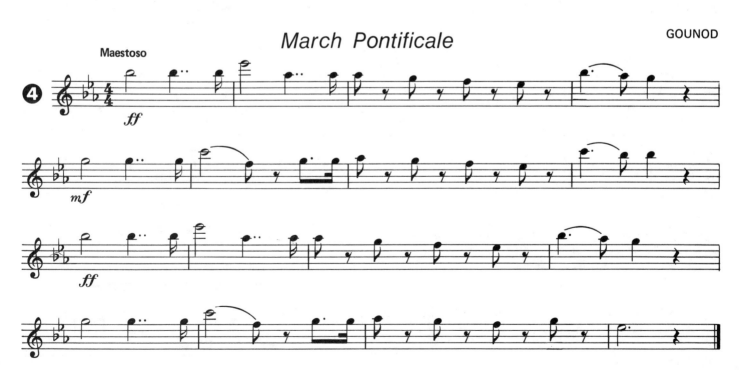

B.I.C.301

TONE STUDY

Chromatic Triplets

6/4 METER

Count: 1 2 3   4 5 6   1 2 3   4 5 6   1   2   3   4   5   6   1 & 2 & 3 & 4 5 & 6 &   1 2 3 4 5 6

Etude In F♯ Minor

Practice both   1 2 3   4   5 6   1 2 3   4 5 6
ways: 1   2   1   2

Dramatic Etude

Marziale

TONE STUDY

Articulation Study

Also, try this study 8va (octave higher).   Be sure to use correct fingerings.

Rhythm Etude

Grace Note Study

Polka From "The Bartered Bride"

SMETANA

OCTAVES

Articulation Etude

Practice numbers ② and ③ in both of the keys indicated.

Rhythm Study

The Mordent
(see explanation on page 43)

Moderato (in 2)

*Use special fingering shown in trill chart.

Sixths

Also play:

etc.

Three evenly divided sixteenth notes (triplets) may be played in place of an eighth note:

Mexican Hat Dance

TRADITIONAL

Allegretto

Tone Study

Play each of the above several times, with various articulations.

RHYTHM STUDY

Study In Sixths

Spanish Dance In F Minor

PLOYHAR

Tone Study

Play in both keys with various articulations.

Rhythm Etude

Intermezzo From "L'Arlesienne Suite"

BIZET

B.I.C.301

SIXTHS

Practice slowly at first - then gradually increase tempo.

Rhythm Etude

5/4 METER

Sixth Symphony Theme

TSCHAIKOWSKY

Double Tonguing

To perform rapid tongued passages, a technique called double tonguing can be used with the syllables DU-GU, TU-KU, or DI-KEH (di as in did). Experiment to determine which syllables achieve the light and rapid style needed. Before applying to the flute, practice the syllables verbally:

Du - Gu - Du - Gu - Du - Gu - Du - Gu - Du

Practice slowly at first on various notes; then gradually increase tempo. Be sure the two syllables are even, both in rhythm and in volume. The second syllable will tend to sound weaker, so ocasionally accent it to overcome this:

Also practice in these ways: 1. Using the second syllable only: GU-GU-GU-GU, etc.
2. DU-DU-DU-DU, GU-GU-GU-GU, etc.

Start slowly and then gradually increase the tempo.

Each day look through the book and find studies suitable for double tonguing. Additional Double Tonguing exercises may be found in the supplementary book STUDIES AND MELODIOUS ETUDES, Level III.

Waltz From The Opera "Faust"

GOUNOD

B.I.C.301

34

Tone Study In D Minor

Largo (very slow)

A double sharp (✗) raises the note one whole step.

Theme From "William Tell"

Andante

ROSSINI

espressivo

Triple Tonguing

Experiment with the syllables DU-GU-DU, TU-KU-TU, or DI-KEH-DI (di as in did).

Du - Gu - Du - Gu   etc.

Apply triple tonguing to the following:

Du - Gu - Du - Du - Gu - Du   etc.

Du -Gu - Du -Du - Gu -Du

Apply triple tonguing to various triplet and $\frac{6}{8}$ studies in this book.

Additional Triple Tonguing exercises may be found in the supplementary book
STUDIES AND MELODIOUS ETUDES, Level III.

Tone Study

Practice the two line above in both of the keys indicated.

CHROMATIC STUDY

(in 2)

✗ means repeat the previous measure.

Trill Etude

(see page 42)

Melody From "Il Trovatore"

VERDI

D. C. al Fine

36

bb minor Scale *(Harmonic Form)*

bb minor Scale *(Melodic Form)*

Studies In Syncopation

Moderato

Count: 1 & 2 & 3 & 1 & 2 & 3 &

(in two)

None But The Lonely Heart

TSCHAIKOWSKY

Andante

*A double flat (bb) lowers the note one whole step.

B.I.C.301

SIXTHS

Practice slowly at first -then gradually increase tempo.

Chromatic Study

Articulation Etude

Also double tongue.

Rhythm Etude

Waltz From "Serenade For Strings"

TSCHAIKOWSKY

38

KEY OF G♭ MAJOR

Play with various articulations.

THIRDS

Articulation Study

Legato Etude

Moderato (in 3)

ANDERSON

Alouette

Allegretto

FRENCH CANADIAN FOLK SONG

Fine

B.I.C.301

D. C. al Fine

TONE STUDY
Slowly

Rhythm Study In B♭ Minor

Allegretto

Trill Etude

Moderato

Nocturne

BORODIN

Andante cantabile

Also play in D Major.

Chromatic Etude

Mazurka

SOUSSMANN

Moderato (in 3)

In this etude the beat remains the same throughout.

Rhythm Etude

Moderato

Scale Study In F Minor

Chromatic Scale Study

Intermezzo From "Cavalleria Rusticana"

MASCAGNI

THE TRILL

The upper note of a trill may be either a half step or a whole step above the principal note, depending upon the key signature. If an accidental accompanies the trill sign it alters the upper note.

Trills are frequently concluded with a double grace note:

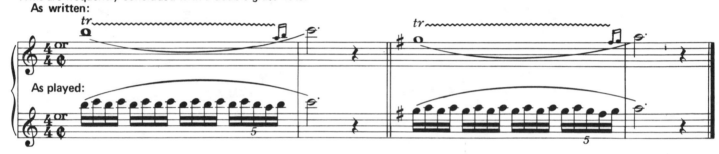

Trills are usually played rapidly but must be played evenly. Be sure the final notes are perfectly controlled.

Several interpretations are used for long trills: 1. Start slowly and gradually increase speed. 2. Play the first two or three notes slowly and then immediately trill rapidly. 3. Play rapidly throughout.

The Turn (Gruppetto)

The turn is a musical ornamentation consisting of four notes including (1) the scale tone above the given note, (2) the given note, (3) the scale tone below the given note, and (4) the given note again. The turn is indicated by this sign ∾ . The turn is executed rapidly near the end of the duration of the given note.

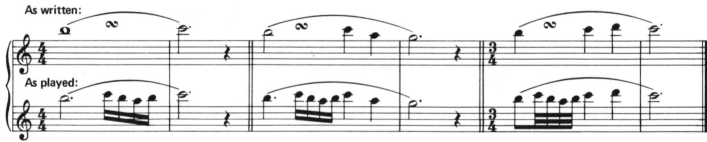

When a turn is to be executed after a dotted note the last note of the turn is given the same value as the dot (Ex. 1). If an accidental is placed over a turn it alters the upper note (Ex. 2). If an accidental is placed under a turn it alters the lower note (Ex. 3). If the turn is placed directly over the given note it is executed very rapidly, starting on the tone above the given note (Ex. 4)

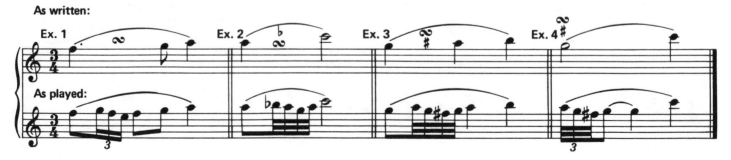

Reference Page

MUSICAL EMBELLISHMENTS
Double And Triple Grace Notes

Groups of more than 3 grace notes are played in a similar manner.

The Long Grace Note

The long grace note (appoggiatura) does not have a dash through its stem and is played on the beat. The long grace note is assigned half the time value of the principal note. However, if it precedes a dotted note, the grace note would receive two-thirds the time value of the principal note. The long grace note usually receives its actual indicated value. You will find this in music composed before the 19th century.

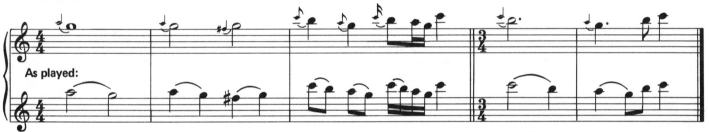

The Mordent

The symbol ∿ over a note means a single trill.

An accidental over the mordent alters the upper note.

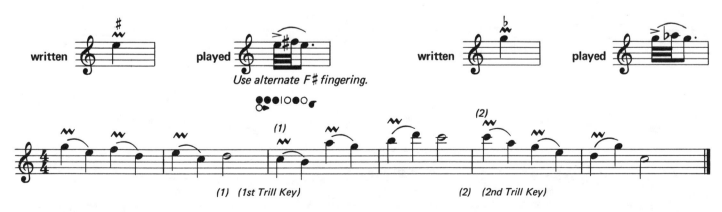

Avoid these wrong interpretations of the mordent: 1. Playing the three notes as a triplet. 2. Playing the first two notes as a double grace note before the beat.

B.I.C.301

Basic Technic For Daily Practice

Start with ANY number and play through the entire pattern, returning to the starting line.
KEEP THE STARTING KEY SIGNATURE THROUGHOUT THE ENTIRE PATTERN.   Use various articulations.